The Washington Monument

Kristin L. Nelson

Lerner Publications Company
Minneapolis

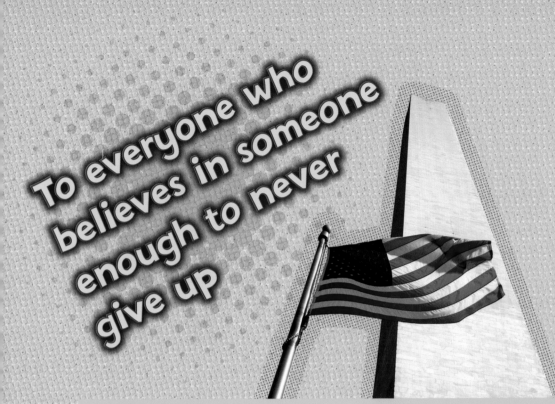

To everyone who believes in someone enough to never give up

Lerner Publications Company
A division of Lerner Publishing Group, Inc.
241 First Avenue North
Minneapolis, MN 55401 U.S.A.

Website address: www.lernerbooks.com

Library of Congress Cataloging-in-Publication Data

Nelson, Kristin L.
      The Washington Monument / by Kristin L. Nelson.
         p.   cm. — (Lightning bolt books™—Famous places)
      Includes index.
      ISBN 978–0–7613–6019–3 (lib. bdg. : alk. paper)
      1. Washington Monument (Washington, D.C.)—Juvenile literature. 2. Washington, George,
1732–1799—Monuments—Washington (D.C.)—Juvenile literature. 3. Washington (D.C.)—Buildings,
structures, etc.—Juvenile literature. I. Title.
   F203.4.W3N46 2011
   975.3—dc22   2009043669

Manufactured in the United States of America
1 — BP — 7/15/10

Contents

Welcome to the Washington Monument

What is the tallest stone building in Washington, D.C.?

It is the Washington Monument.

The Washington Monument glows against a sunset in Washington, D.C.

The monument was built to honor George Washington. He is known as the father of our country.

Why Washington?

In the 1770s, Great Britain ruled America. Americans fought a war for their freedom. George Washington led their army.

George Washington stands bravely in this famous American painting.

The Americans won the war.
The United States became a
new country.

American soldiers
fire at the British.

Washington was elected the first president of the United States.

Washington promises to serve the United States.

Americans named the capital city for George Washington. It was named Washington, D.C.

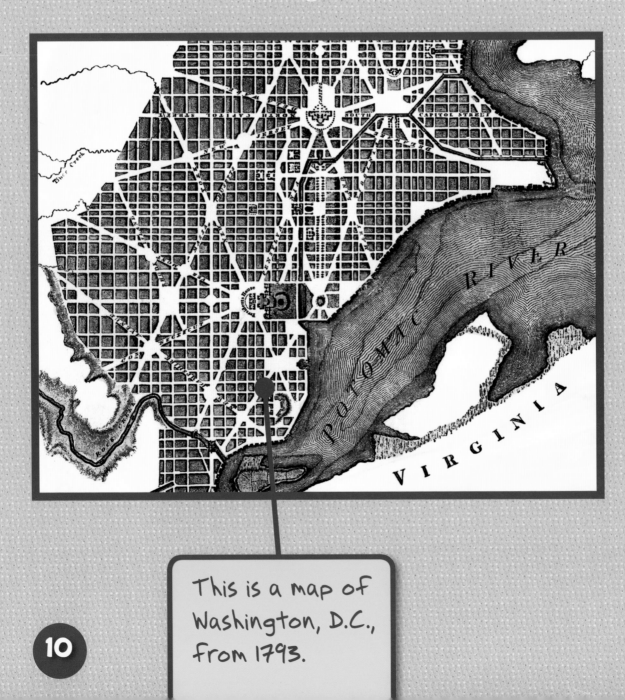

This is a map of Washington, D.C., from 1793.

Building the Washington Monument

Years later, Americans wanted to build a monument to honor Washington. It would be a symbol of their leader's strength.

Washington looks proud in his military uniform.

In 1845, Robert Mills was hired to plan the monument.

He planned an obelisk tower rising out of a round building. An obelisk is square at the bottom. It has a point at the top.

The first plans for the Washington Monument included a round base.

13

Workers began to build the tower in 1848. They used a stone called marble.

Oxen helped haul the heavy marble blocks to the building site.

In a few years, money ran out.
The workers stopped building.

The monument stood
unfinished for years. But
work began again in 1878.

Do you see the ring around the monument? The ring shows where the workers started building again.

The darker and lighter sections on the Washington Monument were built at different times.

Workers could not find the marble used before. So they used a different marble.

Visitors watch as the building of the Washington Monument continues.

The workers only built the obelisk tower. The round building was never made.

Workers build the pointy tip of the Washington Monument.

Inside, the workers
built a stairway to
the top. They built
an elevator too.

People from around the world gave memorial stones. The stones were placed in the walls of the stairway.

There is a stone for every state. Other stones inside the monument help people remember cities or countries.

In 1884, the monument was finally finished!

This is the finished monument as it looked in 1905.

Visiting the Washington Monument

About one million people visit the Washington Monument every year.

Visitors check out the monument from the far end of the Reflecting Pool. This pool lies west of the monument.

At the bottom of the monument, fifty flags wave.

They stand for the fifty states.

Visitors take the elevator to go from the bottom to the top. The elevator has glass doors so you can see the memorial stones in the stairway.

Visitors wait in line for the elevator ride to the top of the monument.

25

At the top of
the monument,
you can see
all around
Washington, D.C.

Here's the view
from the top of
the Washington
Monument.

The Washington Monument stands tall and strong, like our country's first president.

Washington, D.C., Area

UNITED STATES

Maryland
Virginia

Miles

0 — .25 — .5

0 — .25 — .5 — .75

Kilometers

Pennsylvania Avenue

N

White House

Pennsylvania Avenue

Reflecting Pool

NATIONAL MALL

Jefferson Drive

Madison Drive

U.S. Capitol

✳

Washington Monument

POTOMAC RIVER

WASHINGTON, D.C.

VIRGINIA

PENNSYLVANIA

MARYLAND

ATLANTIC OCEAN

WEST VIRGINIA

WASHINGTON, D.C.

VIRGINIA

Fun Facts

- The Washington Monument is 555 feet (169 meters) high. That is twice as tall as the U.S. Capitol Building.

- If the winds are strong enough, the monument sways slightly.

- Lightning struck the monument a year after it was completed. Only one of the outside stones was damaged. But some equipment inside the monument had to be replaced.

- Between 1997 and 2001, workers cleaned the monument. They made it look like new.

Glossary

capital: a city where a government is based. Washington, D.C., is the capital of the United States.

marble: a hard stone with colored patterns in it. It is used for buildings and sculptures.

memorial stone: a stone engraved with words to remind people of a place, a person, an organization, or an event

monument: a building or a statue that reminds people of an event or a person

obelisk: a four-sided pillar with a point at the top

president: the leader of a country, such as the United States

symbol: something that stands for something else

Further Reading

Enchanted Learning: Washington Monument
http://www.enchantedlearning.com/history/us/monuments/washingtonmonument

Hayden, Kate. *Amazing Buildings.* New York: DK Publishing, 2003.

Jango-Cohen, Judith. *Mount Rushmore.* Minneapolis: Lerner Publications Company, 2011.

National Park Service: Washington Monument
http://www.nps.gov/wamo/index.htm

Nelson, Robin. *George Washington: A Life of Leadership.* Minneapolis: Lerner Publications Company, 2006.

Penner, Lucille Recht. *Liberty!: How the Revolutionary War Began.* New York: Random House, 2002.

Piehl, Janet. *The Capitol Building.* Minneapolis: Lerner Publications Company, 2010.

Index

Photo Acknowledgments

The images in this book are used with the permission of: © Markross/Dreamstime.com, p. 2; © Dave Newman/Dreamstime.com, p. 4; © Matthew Carroll/Dreamstime.com, p. 5; © SuperStock/SuperStock, pp. 6, 7; Library of Congress, pp. 8 (LC-USZ62-100726), 9, 15 (LC-DIG-npcc-28308); © North Wind Picture Archives, pp. 10, 18, 20; © Christie's Images/SuperStock, pp. 11, 27; Dictionary of American Portraits, p. 12; © MPI/Hulton Archive/Getty Images, p. 13; © Three Lions/Hulton Archive/Getty Images, p. 14; National Archives, pp. 16 (596327), 19 (596332); © Ping Amranand/SuperStock, p. 17; © Rick Latoff/Photri, p. 21; © Brown Brothers, p. 22; © Pixtal Images/Photolibrary, p. 23; © IndexStock/SuperStock, p. 24; © JAMAL A. WILSON/AFP/Getty Images, p. 25; © Robert Harding Picture Library/SuperStock, p. 26; © Laura Westlund/Independent Picture Service, p. 28; © Nick Edens/Dreamstime.com, p. 29; © Dangerjacob/ Dreamstime.com, p. 30; © Imagez/Dreamstime.com, p. 31.

Cover: © Imagez/Dreamstime.com